Baron von Steuben: The Life and Legacy of the Prussia[n] Drilled the Continental Army at Valley Forge during the Revolutionary War

By Charles River Editors

About Charles River Editors

Charles River Editors is a boutique digital publishing company, specializing in bringing history back to life with educational and engaging books on a wide range of topics. Keep up to date with our new and free offerings with this 5 second sign up on our weekly mailing list, and visit Our Kindle Author Page to see other recently published Kindle titles.

We make these books for you and always want to know our readers' opinions, so we encourage you to leave reviews and look forward to publishing new and exciting titles each week.

Introduction

A statue of von Steuben at Valley Forge

Baron von Steuben

"You say to your soldier, 'Do this' and he does it. But I am obliged to say to the American, 'This is why you ought to do this' and then he does it." – attributed to Baron von Steuben

Many Americans labor under the misconception that the nation's colonial and national heritage was almost wholly accomplished by an English migration, and the notion of early American diversity ends at an acknowledgment of the slave trade conducted between Southern buyers, Northern shippers, the African continent and the Caribbean region. However, early America witnessed the development of New York by the Dutch, the southernmost regions by Spain, and what would become eastern Canada by the French after lengthy battles with Britain. In fact, the Seven Years' War during the 1750s was fought on a nearly global scale between several European belligerents.

As a result, when the Revolution began, the Continental Army sported numerous volunteers from Ireland, Scotland, virtually every European nation between France and Russia, and men from the northern and southern borders of the European continent. There are good reasons America doesn't possess a constitutionally-confirmed national language, despite an English-speaking majority; among the early proposals for such a common language, German and French served as contenders, with the latter going on to become Western Europe's official diplomatic language. Likewise, those who accomplished the legislative, diplomatic, and military miracles that helped 13 separate colonies hold off the greatest power in the world represented a multi-national heritage.

By the time the Revolutionary War started, military confrontations between the world powers had become so common that combat was raised to the status of a fine art, consuming a large portion of time for adolescent males in training and comprising a sizeable component of the economy. Weaponry was developed to a degree of quality not accessible to most North Americans, and European aristocrats were reared in the mastery of swordsmanship with an emphasis on the saber for military use. Likewise, the cavalry, buoyed by a tradition of expert horsemanship and saddle-based combat, was a fighting force largely beyond reach for colonists, which meant that fighting on horses was an undeveloped practice in the fledgling Continental Army, and the American military did not yet fully comprehend the value of cavalry units. Few sword masters were to find their way to North America in time for the war, and the typical American musket was a fair hunting weapon rather than a military one. Even the foot soldier knew little of European military discipline.

However, with European nations unceasingly at war, soldiers from one side or the other often found themselves in disfavor, were marked men in exile, or were fleeing from a superior force. To General George Washington's good fortune, a few found their way to the colonies to join in the cause. Some were adventurers recently cut off from their own borders, while others embraced the American urge for freedom that so closely mirrored the same movements in their home countries.

Autocrats of the 18th century feared an emerging model from the Revolutionary War that might be refashioned by dissidents within their own colonies. Among those living the consequences of defeat and exile, the soldier class of Europe paid particularly close attention. Some were rapt by the growing ideology of the Enlightenment movement as it pertained to their own cultures while others grew weary of inertia imposed by an inability to practice their craft. This brought the participation of various Polish officers who were fleeing the catastrophic result of their rebellion against Russia, including Kasimir Pulaski, who brought with him the prototypical model of the new American cavalry, and Tadeusz Kosciuszko, who as an engineer designed the ramparts of West Point, then fought ably as a cavalryman and commanding officer.

German participation is historically noted for the Hessians, mercenary soldiers recruited in whole companies by Britain, whose standing army featured relatively low numbers when the American Revolution began. However, other Germans noted for their mastery of the science of war sided with the colonies, and among the most essential European contributors to the American cause turned out to be a Prussian officer of German descent. Though he hailed from dubious lineage, he enjoyed the full title of Baron Friedrich Wilhelm Rudolf Gerhard Augustin von Steuben, and when he came to fight in the Revolution, his purportedly lustrous military credentials could not be accurately verified by the American liaisons who were in contact with him. Like the Marquis de Lafayette before him, von Steuben came to Washington's army via the recommendation of Benjamin Franklin, who hoped to use their appointments to curry political favor internationally. Furthermore, the letters sent with von Steuben to America underwent such upgrades of prestige and glamorization as to frame his introduction as a national deceit.

Despite the wavering attention paid by the colonial representatives to his biography, von Steuben may well have contributed more to the rebel victory than any other single presence on the American continent. After another disappointing year of defeats in 1777, Washington's 11,000 men entered winter quarters at Valley Forge in Pennsylvania, about 20 miles outside of occupied Philadelphia. His army had repeatedly faced a lack of discipline and chronic disorganization, and Congress began to consider replacing Washington, who was understandably devastated. Making matters worse, the winter was unusually harsh, leading to an estimated 2,000 or so deaths in camp from diseases. Gouverneur Morris would later call the soldiers at Valley Forge a "skeleton of an army...in a naked, starving condition, out of health, out of spirits."

However, it was at Valley Forge that Washington truly forged his army, most notably by implementing a more rigorous training program for his troops that was led by von Steuben, who had fought with Frederick the Great. Despite speaking little English, von Steuben went about drafting a drill manual in French, and he personally presided over training drills and military parades. With the help of von Steuben, the Continental Army left Valley Forge in the spring of 1778 a more disciplined army than ever before, and the worst of Washington's failures were behind him. Von Steuben would continue to serve with the Continental Army through the end of the war, and he remains one of the most famous officers of the Revolution.

Baron von Steuben: The Life and Legacy of the Prussian General Who Drilled the Continental Army at Valley Forge during the Revolutionary War profiles one of the Revolutionary War's most famous soldiers. Along with pictures of important people, places, and events, you will learn about Baron von Steuben like never before.

Baron von Steuben: The Life and Legacy of the Prussian General Who Drilled the Continental Army at Valley Forge during the Revolutionary War

Von Steuben's Time in Europe

Friedrich Wilhelm von Steuben was born in the German fortress city of Magdeburg in 1730 to a family closely connected to the military, and in service to heads of state. The baron's father was Augustine Steuben, whose name interchangeably employed the obligatory "von," indicative of a figurehead tied to significant property and social prestige. He served Tsarina Anna as a lieutenant among the military engineers, and his career took him to Crimea for a time, then to Kronstadt and the Russian war against Turkey under the command of General Burkhard Christoph von Münnich.

Von Steuben's mother, Elizabeth Maria Justina Dorothea von Jagvodin, either carried the association with nobility from her family name or chose to publicly express the adopted prestige of her husband by furthering the ruse. If the title belonged primarily to Elizabeth, the only path by which the future American commander could legitimately claim such prestigious ancestry came through a maternal lineage, not a preferable course of action for one without a true home, but still workable in Europe.

As it happened, however, the maternal lineage was not the only source of apparent nobility, however manufactured. The baron's paternal grandfather, Augustin, was a mere country parson who entertained notions of living a luxurious life of high rank within his ecclesiastical community. In pursuit of the necessary advancement, he concocted a falsified pedigree attaching himself and his family to the unrelated House of Steuben, a strain dating back to the 13th century in separate locales. Despite not rising as high as Augustin's dreams suggested he might, the ploy worked well for several generations to come, with or without the use of "von" as a consistent feature of the Steuben name. Regardless, the collective family occupied a high social position, as Frederick the Great agreed to be named among the child's godfathers. Baptized as a Calvinist in a largely catholic world, von Steuben was born into royal favor.

The younger von Steuben spent much of his youth visiting various European cultures as part of his father's entourage, not in an educational regimen, but by following the major wars across the continent. He returned to Prussia with his father at the age of 10, and he was already quite astute when it came to military matters. If anything, the future baron came to know little else other than military matters throughout his childhood. Devoid of gentler subjects common to peacetime study, his brain seized on all things connected to "guns, drums, trumpets, fortifications, drills, and parades."[1]

Educated in Breslau and in Neisse of Lower Silesia, Friedrich Wilhelm spent time in Crimea as well before entering a Jesuit School and the University of Breslau. The rigorous training offered by the Catholic order, regardless of the repugnance in which his own faith was held, aided von

---

[1] Review by North American Review of Friedrich Kapp's The Life of Frederick von Steuben, Major-General in the Revolutionary Army, *North American Review*, Vol. 99 No. 205 (Oct., 1864) pp321=365, University of Northern Iowa

Steuben in preparing for military training, which began at the age of 14. In academic studies, he was allowed only to spend time with mathematics and "practical" sciences, pursuits in which disciplined approaches were employed to solve tangible and societally relevant problems rather than wasting time on the purely theoretical or abstract. As a result, von Steuben took little interest in art or organized religion, admiring instead an era of skeptics among the Enlightenment philosophers, including Voltaire, Rousseau, and Diderot.

The pace of von Steuben's early studies and training received a jolt when his godfather, Frederick the Great, invaded the region of Bohemia (presently the Czech Republic). Among Frederick's greatest talents was his ability to effectively reorganize entire states, as he had with Prussia, and by this time, the Prussian military powerhouse encompassed the Germanic states and overlapped into Poland and other central European entities. Von Steuben found himself as an officer in Frederick's ranks by the age of 17, having entered the royal service as a Lance Corporal three years prior. Like his sovereign, he showed an immediate aptitude as an "adept organizer,"[2] a talent that was fostered by an assignment to Frederick's headquarters. There, he was privy to a class in important military processes taught by the king himself, using his own reorganization as a model. The class was a private affair, intended for a small pool of officers who demonstrated the necessary aptitude for high-level military analysis. Some from wealthy, powerful families were in line to avail themselves of the opportunity, but von Steuben was singled out for his talent and zeal. Von Steuben's lessons in Prussian military principles at the hands of its master placed him in what he would deem a core group of instructors who could subsequently spread the information out to others.

[2] Thoughtco., American Revolution: Baron Friedrich von Steuben – www.thoughtco.com/baron-friedrich-von-steuben-2360603

Frederick the Great

The Prussian social and military systems fit von Steuben perfectly. The state spent more than 75% of its entire budget on military resources, and Prussia was commonly described as an "army with a country"[3] and a "latter-day Sparta."[4] In his experience following Frederick the Great at close quarters through his various battles, von Steuben experienced armed conflicts in which the collective sides involved more than 120,000 active combatants. With an immense body of military knowledge gleaned in his young years from such epic collisions, he stood bravely in the trenches through the Siege of Prague in May 1756, during which Frederick, despite being greatly outnumbered, was ultimately victorious. Twice wounded during the campaign, the teenaged officer served in one of his first managerial capacities under the renowned General Hans Sigismund von Lestwitz, in the regiment named for its commander. Lestwitz was later to cast a decidedly negative vote on the young soldier's prospects, declaring that he was "no good as a manager, but clever."[5]

---

[3] Paperdue.com, Baron von Steuben, Friedrich Wilhelm Augustus von Essay – wwwpaperdue.com/baron-von-steuben-friedrich-wilhelm-augustus-84489

[4] Paperdue.com

[5] Stephen C. Danckert, A Genius for Training, Baron von Steuben and the Training of the Continental Army, *Army History* No. 17 (Winter, 1990/1991) U.S. Army Center of Military History, pp 7-10.

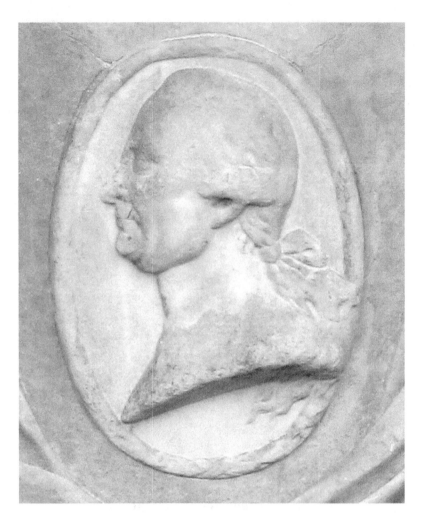

An engraving of von Lestwitz

By 1758, von Steuben was serving under General Johann von Mayr as an adjutant and principle staff officer in a special detached corps. Mayr's *Freibattalion* was by reputation prone to taking risks and was considered quite reckless, thus attracting adventurous soldiers who sought thrills. Specializing in raiding parties, Mayr's units scored many successes against unfavorable odds in surprise engagements.

Upon the death of Mayr in 1759, von Steuben served under General Johann von Hülsen as the commander's aide-de-camp. His notable action during this period came at the Battle of Liegnitz on August 15, 1760. Von Steuben had by this time been promoted to the rank of First Lieutenant. Barely recovered from a wound in the previous year at Kunersdorf, he suffered a second injury at Liegnitz. There, Frederick divided his army into two parts, and when he thought that he heard the other half entering into engagement, he sent 10 battalions into the woods for support. It was a rare mistake on Frederick's part, and the Austrians under Ernst Gideon von Laudon cut down 5,000 Prussian troops in the first 30 minutes. However, Prussia eventually won the artillery duel, and the Austrian troops decided not to continue the assault. Once the regiments were reconstituted, von Steuben took up his position again with "the knowledge of the management of light infantry, [and] a habit of cool and prompt decision in the tumult of battle."[6]

In the summer of 1761, von Steuben was transferred to the general headquarters as a staff officer and Deputy Quartermaster for General von Knobloch at Treptow. In this borough (in the vicinity of present-day Berlin) on the 18th century Russian front, von Knobloch was badly beaten and was compelled to surrender. Von Steuben, experiencing surrender and incarceration for the first time, was called upon to negotiate the terms of surrender and articles of capitulation. Due to his efforts, soldiers were allowed to keep their own clothes, and officers kept their swords.

In von Steuben's case, his term spent as a prisoner of war was by comparison "a pleasant one."[7] The Grand Duke Peter looked upon him with favor and found useful activities for his talents as an envoy. Officers serving under the Tsarina Elizabeth took note of von Steuben's abilities in such matters, so he was chosen by his captors to carry messages to King Frederick. Released in 1762, he returned to service in Prussia, this time as the aide-de-camp for the Prussian king himself, having been promoted to the rank of captain.

However, at the age of 33, von Steuben was abruptly discharged from the Prussian army on April 29, 1763 under mysterious circumstances. On the staff of General Wilhelm von Gaudi following the Treaties of Paris and Hubertsburg, he claimed that his distaste for a general from the Duchy of Anhalt had led to retaliation against him.

Despite other avenues of investigation into his sudden departure from the Prussian service, von Steuben's civilian career began, and it proceeded in a promising manner. Entering the service of Hohenzollern-Hechingen, he renewed a special relationship with Frederick the Great's family. With its castle along the Jüra River flowing out of Lithuania at Baden-Württemberg, he attained the rank of Grand Marshal at the court of the Prince of Hohenzollern-Hechingen. It was during this period that he met Claude Louis, Comte de Saint-Germain, who would become the French Minister of War in the months leading up to the American Revolution, in Hamburg. The count would prove to be critical when it came to recruiting European officers during the Revolution.

[6] North American Review
[7] North American Review

Comte de Saint-Germain

During his term of service in Hohenzollern, von Steuben also served as Colonel of the Swabian Circle and honorary commander of the local militia. Continuing to serve as an envoy, his background prevented political snags with the West, and France in particular. To send French officers for such a purpose was considered a "breach of neutrality,"[8] whereas the use of Prussian officers was fine.

By 1764, von Steuben occupied not only the position of Hofmarschall, but that of Chamberlain to the Petty Court of Hohenzollern-Hechingen. This was largely due to the continued benefits of his ancestor's falsified ancestry, further embroidered by his father during his ascendancy. A few years later, on May 26, 1769, von Steuben was awarded the *Star of the Order of Fidelity* by the

[8] Kevin W. Wright, Friedrich Wilhelm Steuben, Bergen County Historical Society – www.gergencountyhistory.org/Pages/gnsteuben.html

Duchess of Württemberg, the niece of Frederick the Great, and of the Margraviate of Baden. Among the highest of the Margraviate's dynastic awards, the medal featured an eight-point Maltese cross with gold balls on each tip. The gold-plated center with white enamel displayed three mountains below three gold "Cs." Von Steuben was seldom seen without the medal for the rest of his life.

By 1771, von Steuben could for the first time legitimately refer to himself as *Freiherr* (Baron), and his grandfather's scheme was at last officially justified. However, von Steuben's life of luxury was not to last, as the House of Hohenzollern sank into a deep state of debt, forcing its incognito prince to travel from one European state to another in search of handouts. Von Steuben was the only courtier of Hohenzollern to follow the prince on his journeys, primarily to France. Failing to find financial relief, the house was eventually destitute, and the prince returned home.

Despite the bleak outlook for the house's survival, von Steuben was caught unawares by being dismissed from service. Rumors circulated suggesting immoral behavior as the cause, involving a series of romantic liaisons with young men, but either way, von Steuben was resigned to search for work while outpacing the spread of the rumors about his sexuality.

Von Steuben's Path to America

When von Steuben was forced to look elsewhere for money, he had several awards and house titles, but he was not a member of the nobility, so a military officer's commission seemed the most likely avenue for a stable income. In vain, he sought a place in the armies of Austria, Baden, France, and Spain, and when those attempts were fruitless, he eventually traveled as far west as Ireland. According to Paul Lockhart's biography of the baron, he was at last summoned from Paris to Karlsruhe by the Margrave of Baden and set out in anticipation of securing a place in the army of his former state. However, upon his arrival, he found not a position, but what he termed serious warnings based on "a horrible, vicious rumor."[9] The accusation suggested a shadow life of "unsavory conduct,"[10] a reference to alleged homosexual relationships with young boys. No evidence of pedophilia or such relationships ever surfaced, so it's unclear whether the allegations had any truth to them. For his part, von Steuben blamed the aspersions on retaliation, referring to "an inconsiderate step and an implacable enemy"[11] whom he had unwisely slighted in his former office.

Regardless of any lack of hard evidence, von Steuben was warned to stay clear of Versailles at all costs, and to maintain a low profile in Paris to avoid attention. In addition to the rumors, the court of Hohenzollern was predominantly Catholic, and many of its members resented the thought of a heretical Protestant occupying such a high position of favor with the prince. Comte de Saint-Germain intervened, giving von Steuben a letter for Pierre Beaumarchais, the French playwright famous for his stories of the anti-royal Figaro, later set to music by Mozart. Beaumarchais, in turn, introduced the baron to Silas Deane and Benjamin Franklin in Paris.

---

[9] Mark Segal, Baron Friedrich Wilhelm von Steuben, The Closet Professor – www.closetprofessor.blogspot.com/2016/07/baron-friedrich-wilhelm-von-steuben.html

[10] Encyclopaedia Britannica, Baron von Steuben, German Military Officer – www.britannica.com/biography/Baron-von-Steuben

[11] Erin Blakemore

Beaumarchais

When American liaison Silas Deane arrived in Paris near the start of the Revolutionary War to promote diplomacy between France and the colonies, he was a member of the First Continental Congress. His work in committees and secret organizations had made the creation of an American navy possible, and his procurement of supplies helped the rebels capture Ticonderoga in 1775. For this, he claims to have been given the nickname of "Ticonderoga."

Deane

Deane arrived in France posing a commercial agent, but he had Congressional approval for his activities, and he thereby went to work lobbying the French. In addition to recruiting privateers to prey upon British shipping, he would begin to "freely hand out"[12] military commissions to foreign officers, including Baron de Kalb and the Marquis de Lafayette.

---

[12] Harry Schenawolf, Major General Baron Johann von de Kalb, 1721-1780, Foreign Soldier, Americn Patriot, July 16, 2013, Revolutionary War Journal – www.revolutionarywarjounal.com/major-general-baron-dekalb/

Lafayette

Eventually, Deane would be suspected of receiving kickbacks from "French thrill-seekers,"[13] and neither Franklin nor Lee shared Deane's enthusiasm for untested soldiers parading as ceremonial officers in the courts of Europe. This would immediately impact von Steuben. To be fair, the American envoys' reluctance was understandable, because European officers typically joined the Continental Army with a presumption of military superiority and social sophistication, and while the former could occasionally be questioned at high levels, the latter was undoubtedly true. American ideals largely departed from the life of extravagant fashion, detailed courtly behavior, and the unquestioned privilege of the social elite. Furthermore, many of the European officers were ostensibly participating in the Revolution for purposes of burnishing their own credentials for further actions in Europe once their side found themselves again in favor, such as Poland's Tadeusz Kościuszko. Those who were temporarily on the losing faction in their country

[13] Mysteries of Canada, Marquis de Lafayette – The Invasion that was not – www.mysteriesofcanada.com/military/marquis-de-lafayette/

endured the unemployed life with great difficulty, and for some the American effort represented a way of remaining fit and mentally occupied. As if that wasn't enough, many of the foreign officers hailing from locations like France and Prussia arrived with no functional use of the English language.

Von Steuben couldn't have known about those barriers, but he was all too familiar with the rumors about his illicit sexual activities, which had followed him to Paris. When he was initially rejected in his first attempt to offer assistance to the Continental Army in America, he recalled leaving the meetings "in disgust."[14] The introduction to Benjamin Franklin was, he believed, a mere formality, after which he would be free to seek a position with Washington's army, freeing himself from any legal actions in Europe. However, the meeting did not go well - Franklin could offer nothing in terms of pay or rank, and to von Steuben's disgust, Franklin behaved with a total lack of deference toward von Steuben.

Franklin

Frustrated by the meeting, von Steuben resolved to return to Germany, and he reminded

---

[14] National Park Service, Valley Forge, General von Steuben – www.nps.gov/vafo/leaarn/historyculture/vonsteuben.htm

anyone who would listen that his godfather Frederick the Great had taken him into his confidence. He brusquely added that no colonial diplomat should speak to him in such a manner, and he declared that he hoped never to hear a word about America again.

However, one more meeting with an important French diplomat, Comte de Vergennes, led von Steuben to consider a second encounter with the Americans. Like Franklin, Comte de Vergennes could not offer specific conditions, but he reminded von Steuben of his destitute condition and legal danger. He advised the baron, "Go, succeed, and you will never regret the step you have taken."[15]

Vergennes

It's unclear how much the threat of prosecution in Europe softened von Steuben's reluctance to deal with the Americans again, but however it happened, a new series of meetings soon took place. Both Deane and Franklin had continued to recruit officers in the first few years of the Revolution, even when instructed to cease and desist by the Continental Congress, and in the summer of 1777, about a year after the Declaration of Independence, von Steuben was "endorsed

[15] North American Review

for service"[16] by Comte de Saint-Germain.

Aware of von Steuben's career from nearly the beginning, Comte de Saint-Germain made a positive note of the baron's long years of meritorious service across Europe and brushed aside any notion that Franklin and Deane were no longer authorized to recruit foreigners. Von Steuben, in his reaction to the first meeting, was ignorant of that development, but Congress had already grown weary of interviewing mercenaries, criminals, and glory seekers with inflated credentials. Franklin's dilemma was that he understood the disorganization of the Continental Army, and he also understood that von Steuben was the right man to improve the situation, but with Congress in such a state, a captain retired for 14 years and late into his best fighting years stood a "scant chance"[17] of securing a commission in Philadelphia.

The second journey to Paris to meet with the American delegation came with a vague offer at best. Through the French count, von Steuben was fully apprised of the opportunities for glory in North America, but while the American representatives offered free passage across the Atlantic, they were still unable to speak to the matter of either rank or pay. Franklin also displayed some hesitation based on the widespread rumors of von Steuben's alleged misconduct, but in the end decided that staffing the Continental Army with experienced officers was more crucial than the candidate's sexuality. With Deane, he set about enhancing von Steuben's value to Congress, and given that von Steuben had been involved in so many Prussian conflicts, the potential to fabricate his experience was enormous. By the time his credentials were presented before Congress, Captain von Steuben had been upgraded to a "Lieutenant General in the King of Prussia's Service."[18] Franklin's diplomatic deceit could have resulted in a catastrophe for the Continental Army, but to everyone's good fortune, the baron's mixture of discipline and eagerness to serve would produce stunning results.

On September 27, 1777, von Steuben and a number of European officers sailed for the colonies from Marseilles, despite the fact France's King Louis XVI, having recently experienced a stinging defeat at the hands of the British, had no desire to further provoke King George III. Likewise, Britain was already angered at the thought of European officers fighting against them regardless of the port of origin, so the British sought to board and seize ships carrying officers from French ports heading west. As an alias, von Steuben sailed under the simple name of Frank, according to the captain's log, and even the ship's name was altered to *Flamand*.

The voyage proceeded largely without incident, and the *Flamand* arrived in Portsmouth, New Hampshire in November 1777. With his Italian greyhound, Azor, a French military secretary under the name of Pierre Etienne Du Ponceau, and aide-de-camp Louis de Pontière, von Steuben created a minor sensation upon his arrival. He had clearly demonstrated a major lack of judgment

---

[16] Historic Valley Forge, Baron von Steuben – www.history.org/valleyforge/served/steuben.html
[17] North American Review
[18] Historic Valley Forge

by outfitting his entourage in bright red uniforms, and he was very nearly arrested by rebel forces operating under the impression that he was British.

Once that was resolved, he traveled overland to Boston, where he met extensively with John Hancock, who had previously been the President of the Continental Congress. For several days and nights, von Steuben was "extravagantly entertained"[19] in Boston as a celebrity far more notable than his real life would suggest. His early experiences in America bordered on the luxurious, and von Steuben took no small pleasure in it. Hancock's retirement from Congress had left him somewhat out of the loop when it came to information, but he was eager to further the war effort. Once he had equipped von Steuben with a sleigh, horses, servants and an extended entourage, he carefully plotted the baron's route to York, the small city to which Congress had temporarily relocated following the British occupation of Philadelphia. Unfortunately, with British patrols throughout the countryside, a circuitous route was required, and the eventual distance to the temporary capital exceeded 400 miles.

Hancock

[19] Historic Valley Forge

Despite the pampering treatment Hancock offered in Boston, he also took the time to inform von Steuben of military and financial realities, and that Congress would likely suffer under the relocation for at least one winter.

Von Steuben's introduction to Congress was well-played; he offered his services as a volunteer, abasing himself as much as possible for an experienced Prussian soldier. His offer undercut the principal pillar by which Congress had rejected so many. In tandem with his appearance, recommendations poured in from Boston and other sources, revealing the news that von Steuben had served as a personal "Apostle"[20] to Frederick the Great himself, and that as an intimate member of the king's family, he was a cherished godson. As he made the rounds to be entertained by the leading political figures of the day, the rumors of impropriety surfaced briefly, causing a rift with John Adams and his family. It was alleged that von Steuben carried on a brief relationship with Charles Adams, John's son. Little was said of the matter publicly, but Abigail noted that her son was "not at peace with himself,"[21] adding that Charles was "infatuated with and adored von Steuben."[22] Whatever happened, the purported relationship appears to have been well-contained, and it created no ramifications for von Steuben's career. Charles did not live past the age of 30, succumbing to cirrhosis of the liver.

In time, the niceties of socializing with public figures gave way to the reality of service, and von Steuben eagerly anticipated the opportunity to begin his work by joining Washington's Continental Army at Valley Forge. As he began the final leg from York, he passed through the Lancaster country of Pennsylvania, causing an uproar of civic pride among the large German population there.

Valley Forge

Von Steuben had arrived in America at a precarious time for the rebel cause. Washington is now the most famous American in history and is viewed as his country's greatest Revolutionary hero, but he and his Continental Army had a terrible year after the British evacuated Boston in March 1776. At the end of 1776, the American war effort was on the verge of collapse, and despite Washington's success during the surprise attack at Trenton, the British were confident that they could quell the rebellion in 1777. That winter, the British planned a complicated campaign in which British armies from Canada and New York would strike out across New England and link up, with the goal of cutting off the Northern colonies. 1777 would prove to be the pivotal year of the war, but not in the way the British intended.

---

[20] Study.com, Baron von Steuben – www.study.com/academy/lesson/baron-von-steuben-quotes-facts-biography.htm
[21] Mark Segal
[22] Mark Segal

Washington as leader of the Continental Army

The British planned a three-pronged sweep through the northern colonies that would eventually end with the linking of three different forces. The design of the plan called for the capture of Philadelphia, as well as the colony of New York, and it aimed all but slice the rebellious colonies in two.

The main thrust of the campaign was John Burgoyne's army of nearly 8,000 men, which started out from Quebec and began making its way south through New York. From the beginning, however, Burgoyne was not on the same page as William Howe. Burgoyne had concocted the campaign strategy and received approval from an intermediary. However, Howe had informed that same intermediary that he could not meet up with Burgoyne in New York because he calculated he would be busy late into the year taking Philadelphia. It's unclear whether Burgoyne was ever informed of Howe's response, but unbeknownst to each other, the two commanders were not on the same page.

Burgoyne

By July, Burgoyne had taken Fort Ticonderoga in New York, but as he tried to get a bearing on the coordinated strategy, the Americans shot another hole into the grand campaign at Fort Stanwix.

The British and their Native American allies had inflicted some serious damage on militiamen near Fort Stanwix, but General Benedict Arnold led an 800 man contingent to the outskirts of the fort and began to lay siege. Realizing that he would not win an open battle, Arnold resorted to subterfuge and succeeded into fooling the British allied Native Americans that he had a much larger force. When the British were left without their allies, Colonel Anthony St. Leger decided head back toward Quebec. His men would never link up with Burgoyne's as planned.

At the end of August, Burgoyne learned that St. Leger would not be linking up with him, and that he could not expect help from Howe near New York City or Philadelphia. Nevertheless, while worried about where he would camp his army for the winter, Burgoyne decided to keep advancing in September. Thus, instead of heading back to Ticonderoga, Burgoyne made Albany his target for winter camping, and he ordered his army forward until they were just a few miles north of Saratoga by mid-September.

In September 1777, Burgoyne's advance was opposed by nearly 10,000 Americans led by General Horatio Gates, who had taken over for Philip Schuyler. Under the advice of the renowned Polish engineer Tadeusz Kościuszko, Gates anchored his army's line from the Hudson River to bluffs known as Bemis Heights. Gates assumed direct command of the army's right wing, and he put Arnold in command of the left wing, which was stationed on Bemis Heights. Though the two had gotten along earlier in the war and Gates had been one of Arnold's strongest allies, he was apparently rubbed the wrong way when Arnold chose Schuyler allies for his staff. Gates despised Schuyler, and this led to animosity between Gates and Arnold as well due to both generals' obstinate personalities.

Gates

During the First Battle of Saratoga, fought on September 19, Burgoyne's army moved to flank Arnold, who had anticipated an attack on his wing and had asked Gates to allow him to position his troops on Freeman's Farm to block a potential flank attack. Gates, however, anticipated a frontal assault and thus only allowed Arnold to send a small contingent of Daniel Morgan's riflemen and other light infantry to reconnoiter in that vicinity. As it turned out, that reconnaissance came into contact with Burgoyne's flank, starting the Battle of Freeman's Farm. Although the British won a tactical victory, the Americans inflicted nearly 600 casualties, about 10% of Burgoyne's effective fighting force.

Understandably, Arnold was miffed that the result took place because his advice had been ignored, and it boiled over into an all out feud with Gates, who conspicuously refused to mention Arnold at all in the official account of the battle. At the same time, Gates removed Morgan's company from Arnold's command, bringing about a vocal shouting match between Gates and Arnold that resulted in Gates sidelining Arnold and telling him he was being replaced in command of that wing.

After the argument, Arnold began preparing to formally request a transfer to George Washington's command, while Gates continued to humiliate Arnold at the camp. It's still unclear why Arnold continued to stay with Gates's army, but it proved to be one of the most fortuitous decisions of the American Revolution.

Unbeknownst to the Americans at the time, Burgoyne was in contact with British General Sir Henry Clinton over whether Clinton could move diversionary forces in time to assist Burgoyne. Burgoyne went so far as to explain to Clinton that he would be forced to retreat by early October without reinforcements. As fate would have it, Clinton would actually begin moving forces that way and take some forts in the vicinity in early October, but his messengers announcing that to Burgoyne were captured. Burgoyne wouldn't learn about Clinton's movements until after the Battle of Bemis Heights.

In early October, the demoted Arnold got into one more argument with Gates after proposing an advance against the British. By this time, Gates had taken command of the left wing and promptly informed Arnold, "You have no business here." At the same time, when General Lincoln proposed similar advice, Gates took it and followed it. With a plan to attack both British flanks, the Battle of Bemis Heights started with the American advance on the left coming into contact with the British. The Americans began making progress on both sides of the British line, and British General Simon Fraser was mortally wounded on their right flank, helping the American cause.

As gunfire could be heard back at camp, Arnold only got more agitated at his situation. Unable to stand being sidelined any more, Arnold took off toward the right, where Enoch Poor's column was attempting to flank the British left. With this obvious defiance of orders and complete insubordination, Gates sent an aide after Arnold to bring him back to camp.

Thankfully, that aide, Major Armstrong, was unable to do so. To every soldier's surprise, General Arnold was soon spotted at the front leading the attack on a British redoubt. Arnold was so worked up that some believed he had been drinking. The British had been able to hold the redoubt with such spirit that Burgoyne wrote after the battle, "A more determined perseverance than they showed ... is not in any officer's experience." However, it would be Arnold who persevered, and he led another charge through a gap between two British redoubts, allowing American troops to threaten the rear of British General Breymann's men in the redoubt. Showing absolutely no concern for his well-being, Arnold rode his horse up and down the line inbetween the Americans and British. During the attack, Breymann was killed and the Americans captured the redoubt, but near the end of the fighting, one of the final volleys hit Arnold in his leg and his horse, who fell onto the same leg and broke it.

By the time the decisive American victory was finished, Burgoyne had lost nearly 20% of his effective fighting during the battles at Saratoga, and after a few days his trapped army surrendered to the Americans.

The French had refused to provide more than arms and money throughout 1777, until they learned in December 1777 about Saratoga and Burgoyne's surrender. With that news, French King Louis XVI entered into a formal military alliance with the United States, and in February 1778, France joined the war. Naturally, the accolades for Saratoga went to Gates as commanding general, while the grievously wounded Arnold would be recommissioned Major General Arnold with his proper relative rank restored. Even still, Gates failed to credit Arnold for the success at Saratoga, and his actions also came at an incredible cost: his leg was so shattered that doctors wanted to amputate it, failing to do so only at the threat of physical violence by Arnold himself. By setting the leg, it would remain 2 inches shorter than Arnold's other leg for the rest of his life. Arnold would be out of service for nearly half a year, and he would never truly be physically fit again. The path that would lead to his notorious betrayal of the cause was set.

Though Americans would be able to look back in hindsight at 1777 as the year the American Revolution reached a turning point in favor of the colonists, the winter of 1777 was still considered a miserable point for the cause at the time. Although Benedict Arnold and Horatio Gates were victorious at Saratoga, Washington and his army had been less successful. After being pushed back into Pennsylvania at the end of 1776, Washington attempted to surround the British army as it invaded Philadelphia in 1777, but he failed miserably. At the Battle of Germantown, Washington was defeated and forced to retreat, and on October 19, 1777, the British entered Philadelphia and the Continental Congress fled to nearby York. Ultimately, it would be the French, not Washington, who forced the British out of Philadelphia; after learning of the French entry into the war, the British immediately abandoned Philadelphia to garrison New York City, which the British feared could be taken by French naval assault.

In looking for a place to establish his winter camp, Washington came across a small community known as Valley Forge. Located 20 miles northwest of Philadelphia, it seemed like an ideal location; there was plenty of empty land around the village in which his men could build shelters, and it was close enough to the British lines to keep an eye on their movements while being far enough away to keep them from attacking in force.

If anything, Washington made his winter camp just in time, because his army was in desperate need. To illustrate this point, the following story was later told: "The officer commanding the detachment, choosing the most favorable ground, paraded his men to pay their General the honors of a passing salute. As Washington rode slowly up, he was observed to be eying very earnestly something that attracted his attention on the frozen surface of the road. Having returned the salute with that native grace and dignified manner that won the admiration of the soldiers of the Revolution, the Chief reined in his charger, and ordering the commanding officer of the detachment to his side, addressed him as follows: 'How comes it, sir, that I have tracked the march of your troops by the blood-stains of their feet upon the frozen ground? Were there no shoes in the commissary's stores that this sad spectacle is to be seen along the public highway?' The officer replied: 'Your Excellency may rest assured that this sight is as painful to my feelings as it can be to yours, but there is no remedy within our reach. When shoes were issued the different regiments were served in turn; it was our misfortune to be among the last to be served, and the stores became exhausted before we could obtain even the smallest supply.' The General was observed to be deeply affected by his officer's description of the soldiers' privations and sufferings. His compressed lips, the heaving of his manly chest betokened the powerful emotions that were struggling in his bosom, when, turning towards the troops, with a voice tremulous, yet kindly, he exclaimed, 'poor fellows!' Then giving rein to his horse he rode rapidly away."

A picture of the perimeter of the camp looking southeast towards Philadelphia

A picture of a cannon and redan pointed southeast towards the British lines at Philadelphia

When Washington and his men finally arrived at Valley Forge, they found little to welcome them. While a few of the townspeople surrendered their homes or at least a room or two for the officers' use, the vast majority of the men had to build their own shelter. This may not have been as bad as it sounds given that most of them had built homes in the wilderness before, but the terrible weather made their task both urgent and daunting.

Washington was respectful of the needs of the farmers living around him, but he knew the army was fighting for their freedom and thus had no qualms demanding that they do their part. On December 20, he ordered, "By virtue of the power and direction especially given, I hereby enjoin and require all persons residing within seventy miles of my headquarters to thresh one-half of their grain by the first day of March next ensuing, on pain, in case of failure, of having all that shall remain in sheaves, after the period above mentioned, seized by the Commissaries and Quartermasters of the army, and paid for as straw."

Replicas of the cabins constructed for common soldiers

Pictures of the replicated inside of common soldiers' cabins at Valley Forge

While his men were building huts and establishing their homes for the next six months, Washington was busy establishing order in the camp. To that end, on December 22, 1777, he published the General Orders for the camp. His first concern was to hang on to his soldiers, many of whom were growing discouraged and considering desertion. Moreover, some reasoned that if they were going to stay in the same place for the winter, they might as well return home and live with their families until it was time to fight again.

Moreover, there was another concern, one that involved both morale and practicality. Washington did not have enough arms for his men, a situation he did not wish to draw attention to, but at the same time, soldiers obviously expected to have weapons.

As December gave way to 1778, the army was becoming increasingly desperate for basic supplies. Even water was in short supply, to the extent the men had to depend on melting snow for drinking. This was a problem, because even though the winter was cold and frosty, there was not a lot of snow. Thus, Washington kept pressing the Continental Congress, trying again to convince the powers that be that the men could not survive, much less fight, unless they were fed: "All I could do under these circumstances was, to send out a few light Parties to watch and harrass the Enemy, whilst other Parties were instantly detached different ways to collect, if possible, as much Provision as would satisfy the present pressing wants of the Soldiery. But will this answer? No Sir: three or four days bad weather would prove our destruction. What then is to become of the Army this Winter? and if we are as often without Provisions now, as with it , what is to become of us in the Spring, when our force will be collected, with the aid perhaps of Militia, to take advantage of an early Campaign before the Enemy can be reinforced?"

Hoping that he had made a point, Washington used uncharacteristically strong language, going so far as to admit that he was tired of being blamed for the incompetence of others: "These are considerations of great magnitude, meriting the closest attention, and will, when my own reputation is so intimately connected, and to be affected by the event, justify my saying that [either] the present Commissaries are by no means equal to the execution [of their Office] or that the disaffection of the People is past all belief. The misfortune however does in my opinion, proceed from both causes, and though I have been tender heretofore of giving any opinion, or lodging complaints, as the change in that department took place contrary to my judgment, and the consequences thereof were predicted; yet, finding that the inactivity of the Army, whether for want of provisions, Clothes, or other essentials, is charged to my Account, not only by the common vulgar, but those in power, it is time to speak plain in exculpation of myself; with truth then I can declare that, no Man, in my opinion, ever had his measures more impeded than I have, by every department of the Army."

That said, seeing his men sleeping night after night on damp, festering ground was enough to anger him, and he enumerated each of the offences against his efforts: "Since the Month of July, we have had no assistance from the Quarter Master Genl. and to want of assistance from this department, the Commissary Genl. charges great part of his deficiency; to this I am to add, that notwithstanding it is a standing order (and often repeated) that the Troops shall always have two days Provisions by them, that they may be ready at any sudden call, yet, no opportunity has scarce[ly] ever yet happened of taking advantage of the Enemy that has not been either totally obstructed or greatly impeded on this Acct., and this…great and crying evil is not all."

Washington then went on to name the many items, other than food, that his men depended on: "Soap, Vinegar and other Articles allowed by Congress we see none of nor have [we] seen [them] I believe since the battle of Brandywine; the first indeed we have now little occasion of [for] few men having more than one Shirt, many only the [half] of one, and Some none at all…"

While the food was an obvious necessity, Washington and his men were facing a long, hard winter during which common soldiers would be sheltered in substandard accommodations. Warm clothes were an obvious necessity, but the army did not have them. At one point, as many as 4,000 men had to report as unfit for duty simply because they did not having enough clothing to cover themselves or shoes to wear.

On January 24, 1778, five representatives from Congress arrived in Valley Forge to assess the situation for themselves and report back their findings, and they were so thoroughly shocked by what they saw that they agreed to Washington's request that the Congress itself take over the purchase and distribution of supplies. Within a month, the situation in camp had improved, at least as far as food and clothes went, but by then, many of the illnesses that resulted due to exposure and overcrowding had taken their toll.

By this time, Washington had lost more men to typhoid, typhus, dysentery and pneumonia than he had to bayonets and bullets. Despite improvements in the army's provisions, the situation at Valley Forge remained desperate, and years later, Chief Justice of the Supreme Court John Marshall observed that at no other time "had the American Army been reduced to a situation of greater peril than during the winter at Valley Forge.

As things took a turn for the worse, many began to criticize Washington and even call for his replacement. Some felt that General Horatio Gates, the hero of the Battle of Saratoga, would do a better job, including Gates himself, who frequently angled for the job by criticizing Washington. Brigadier General Thomas Conway had also been working for some time to undermine Washington, and he was joined in his efforts by Dr. Benjamin Rush, one of the signers of the Declaration of Independence.

Conway

Once the conspiracy to replace Washington was uncovered, Gates was forced to apologize and lost his position on the Board of War, returning to his former command in New York. Conway eventually found himself in an ill-considered duel with General Cadwalader, an admirer of Washington. He challenged the general for a perceived slight upon his honor, and the two met in Philadelphia to conduct the ritual. John Cadwalader shot Conway in the mouth, after which he bragged that the injury could not have been in a better place. Conway would go on to apologize in writing to Washington before returning to France.

On February 12, 1778, General James Varnum conceded "that in all human probability the army must dissolve. Many of the troops are destitute of meat and are several days in arrears. The horses are dying for want of forage. The country in the vicinity of the camp is exhausted. There cannot be a moral certainty of bettering our condition while we remain here, what consequences have we rationally to expect?" That same week, Washington admitted in a letter to Governor George Clinton, "For some days past there has been little less than a famine in camp. A part of the army has been a week without any kind of flesh, and the rest three or four days. Naked and starved as they are, we cannot enough admire the incomparable patience and fidelity of the soldiery, that they have not been, ere this, excited by their sufferings to general mutiny and desertion."

This was the state of affairs when Washington rode out to greet von Steuben himself on February 5, 1778 with a guard of 25 men. The Prussian was somewhat embarrassed by the attention given to a volunteer, which he expressed freely to the commanding general. Washington is said to have replied, "The whole army would stand for sentinel for such volunteers."[23] Skeptical as Washington had grown by new officers attempting to subvert his authority and decisions, he took von Steuben as an officer with a surprising body of military knowledge. Above all, he sensed the Prussian's sincerity, which he took at face value despite some initial hesitation. Rather than expressing scorn at troops in such a condition of squalor, incompetence, and illness, von Steuben found himself "admiring an army which held together under circumstances which no European army could have endured."[24]

Of course, the skepticism on Washington's part was understandable. The man who stood before him was a "paunchy, balding officer in his mid-forties."[25] He held Franklin's recommendation in his hand, but Franklin had been wrong before, and for Washington, a recruiter's mistake could go far beyond the danger experienced in the diplomatic realm. In truth, despite von Steuben's excellent training, the best that can be historically made of Franklin's recommendation was that the recommendation was "mistaken to say the least,"[26] and brutally dishonest. It is true that at the rank of captain, many soldiers led units of troops, but von Steuben had spent much time at such a rank as the king's aide-de-camp. No such experience as a leader was ever located in authentic Prussian archives from the period, and his purported rank of Lieutenant General, bestowed upon him by Franklin and Deane, was "purely fictitious,"[27] an outright lie in pursuit of an optimistic outcome.

Along with the elevated recommendation present in Franklin's letter, von Steuben proceeded to match it with an air of great confidence, and he was able to impress upon Washington his desire to serve out of higher motives. There was nothing of the glory-seeking mercenary to be found in him, and he seemed to express a natural sincerity. As he nearly always did, von Steuben wore the Order of Fidelity on his lapel, and his own introductory letter to Washington stated that it was the Prussian's "greatest ambition…[to] render your country all the Services in my Power, and to deserve the title of Citizen of America by fighting for the cause of your Liberty." Washington responded in his observations to others that von Steuben "appears to be much of a gentleman."[28]

Regardless of first impressions, von Steuben was nevertheless untested, and Washington could not be certain of his prospects for success. To ensure that yet another suspicious foreign unknown was not being thrust upon him, he turned the matter over to Alexander Hamilton, his

---

[23] North American Review

[24] Allen French, Review of John McAuley Palmer's General von Steuben, *The American Historical Review*, Vol. 43 No. 4 (July 1938) pp894-895

[25] Stehen C. Danckert

[26] John McAuley Palmer

[27] John McAuley Palmer

[28] Mount Vernon.org

aide-de-camp, and Hamilton and Nathanael Greene took charge of the newcomer's preparation. In the same vein, the beginning of the baron's service as a Major General in the Continental Army was not without resistance among the ranks, as fellow generals fell at once to disparaging him as a threat. Charles Lee (who was soon to disgrace himself at the Battle of Monmouth Courthouse in New Jersey) and General Thomas Mifflin discredited von Steuben through a whisper campaign that featured much intrigue and precious little substance. Ironically, von Steuben persevered in no small part due to a lack of fluency in English, and, mostly unaware of the rumors going on behind his back, he set about training the troops still at Valley Forge on the most basic level.

Hamilton

Greene

Accustomed to military units trained and outfitted by tradition, even Washington's apologies for the state of the Continental Army could not prepare von Steuben for what he encountered. The Continental Army had been established as a force around Boston only two years prior as an amalgamation of disparate militias and volunteers of various origins. Uniforms and weapons were standardized as best they could be in some areas, but for the most part, soldiers brought what they had. Some weapons were imported, while others were homemade, and of varying degrees of quality. Advantages over the British system were few and far between, but one asset favored the Americans, as those joining the ranks from the frontier brought long rifles, capable of longer ranges than the standard issue British rifle. Employing these weapons for survival in the wilderness, frontiersmen were often found to be superior marksmen as well. British troops were uniformly outfitted with bayonets, but the Americans had little to no experience with the weapon, and it was not easily found among a Continental Army soldier's standard equipment. According to von Steuben, it was more often employed as a tool for roasting meat, and when it came to battle, the colonial soldier "often left it at home."[29] Bemoaning the loss of the bayonet as an effective weapon among his new troops, von Steuben wrote that "the American soldier, never having used this arm, had no faith in it."[30] The Prussian was further dismayed by the American soldiers indifference toward a code of military behavior, and he lamented their clothes, which

[29] James Still, Baron von Steuben (1778), The Post & Mail, February 1, 2018 – www.thepostmail.com/2018/02/01/baron-von-steuben-1778/
[30] James Still

were clearly insufficient for surviving a harsh northern winter.

Already aghast at the sight of "naked troops bearing rusty muskets,"[31] he soon discovered that no unit serving under Washington was capable of waging "linear combat."[32] In terms of marching and battle formations, the militias making up the broader army were incapable of coordinating their systems with one another, and since they were mostly only able to march in single file, the Americans had relied on the guerilla tactics of various Native American tribes, with the backdrop of deep woods for escape and combat. With their bright red coats, British troops who pursued the enemy into dense forests were easy targets, but they soon learned to avoid such pursuit, insisting on fighting in the open field. Once guerilla tactics were removed and the American soldiers were required to come out into the open, the disadvantage was painfully evident. With no common sense for configuring group volleys, a high danger of friendly fire existed, and collective confidence could not be maintained. In his later notes, von Steuben admitted, "With regard to military discipline, I may safely say that no such thing existed in the Continental Army."[33]

Taking stock of his situation, von Steuben formulated a regimen of training, sanitation, and morale-building based on his experiences in Europe, and the changes began with a lesson in basic sanitation. The Americans huddled at Valley Forge lived the life of forest animals, and they had given little thought to improving health conditions. Men relieved themselves wherever they wished, then pitched their tents nearby. Winding through the sea of tents and huts to report for duty was a serpentine affair that would have ended in catastrophe in the case of an emergency. Moreover, kitchens and cooking fires were scattered indiscriminately throughout the encampment.

To deal with all this, von Steuben instituted a system of regimental "streets," through which tents were made more accessible and more cohesively located by unit. Separate streets were designated for infantrymen, officers, and high-ranking officers. Kitchens were situated on the opposite side of the camp to latrines, which were dug downhill from tents in order to keep living areas clean.

Warfare in the 18th century was by modern standards "comparatively simple,"[34] once all the preliminaries of jockeying for position, feints, and impressive displays of royal garb and artillery were out of the way. The true onset of combat generally took place at close range, and the value of volley firing was supreme. A mass of men stood shoulder-to-shoulder firing indiscriminately into a similar mass of enemy soldiers. More important than individual accuracy was a unit's ability to fire, reload, and fire again with great rapidity, snipers being the lone exception. In the

[31] Eric Trickey, The Prussian Nobleman Who Helped Save the American Revolution, Smithsonian.com, April 26, 2017 – www.smithsonian.com/history/baron-von-steuben-18964048

[32] Stephen C. Danckert

[33] Friedrich Wilhelm von Steuben Quotes – www.azquotes.com/author/S1040-Friedrich_Wilhelm_von_Steuben

[34] Historic Valley Forge

contemporary sense, rapid firing did not exist, as no repeating firearms were yet invented. However, the European armies practiced drills on specific rhythmic counts, breaking down the handling of firearms into small components. So adept was the Prussian army in general musket fire that a second volley could be managed in 17 motions set to eight or nine counts.

Von Steuben knew all the necessary tactics, but outfitting the American soldier in a standardized manner was difficult. Few factories existed for producing high quality weaponry, currency was greatly devalued, and the distribution network was primitive, making it generally unreliable for shipping at large distances. Muskets used by both sides had severe limitations, and everyone depended on a "mass-fire melee"[35] for filling the air with lead. However, British muskets were standardized with the manufacture of the "Brown Bess,"[36] reliably firing a one-ounce ball of lead.

Officers of both armies often carried sabers, which could be worn or left at camp depending on the situation. The saber was an integral weapon for the cavalry, but the Continental Army lacked such a force until Casimir Pulaski established the first units. Otherwise, the saber was as much a sign of rank or prestige as it was a weapon.

The Continental soldier occasionally carried more effective small arms such as pistols and spear-like spontoons and halberds. Each infantryman carried a leather or tin container holding 20 to 30 rounds of ammunition. The use of brightly colored uniforms in many European armies has been questioned over the years as a poor example of camouflage, but considering the smoke clouds caused by black powder weapons of the era, recognizing one's own troops was not always guaranteed, so the colors made sense in that context.

Von Steuben was aware of the length of time required to properly train a Prussian soldier, and he knew Washington's troops would be on the march in a period of only 1-2 months. To deal with that reality, simplified the intricate Prussian system to a point where the Americans could progress quickly. With the victory often going to that group able to produce a second volley before the enemy, von Steuben took those most adept at handling a musket and placed them within groups of three as the core of a successful firing line. Eventually, these groups grew to 12.

With the number of weapon-proficient men increasing, a "model company"[37] of 100 was formed. These prototypical combat soldiers, once trained, would serve as instructors, working outward to train each successive brigade. Within a brief period, the entire army passed through this aspect of the training program, and von Steuben himself led the training of the core group, an unusual habit. In the European tradition, officers never got down in the mud to train in a direct relationship with the foot soldier. It was considered "ungentlemanly for officers to do so,"[38] as

---

[35] Historic Valley Forge

[36] J. Lloyd Durham, Outfitting an American Revolutionary Soldier, NCPedia, North Carolina Museum of History, 1992 –
    www.ncpeia.org/history/usrevolution/soldiers

[37] Historic Valley Forge

the distance of command could come under threat. Class distinction was as present in the military as it was in the rest of society, so officers, the army's aristocracy, never mixed with the commoner. Once the model company began to instruct their fellow units in turn, drilling was taken over by non-commissioned officers. The creation of this mid-level leader served as a buffer between officer and infantryman, establishing the sergeant as one of the most essential roles for preparation. The value of the non-commissioned officer holds true to the present day.

The drill process moved slowly at first, with constant marching and musket handling taking up many hours. Von Steuben spoke virtually no English, and in the daily delivery of rants before his troops, not a word was understood. Hamilton and Greene were of some assistance, but eventually, it was Captain Benjamin Walker who saved the day by stepping forward and offering to receive von Steuben's orders in French, translating them to the troops in English. Walker was an English-born accountant with the skills most needed by Washington's army. Von Steuben immediately recognized this, and a lifelong friendship ensued. However, for more immediate purposes, Walker was assigned the task of ranting at individual soldiers in English after von Steuben had tired of "swearing and yelling"[39] in German and French. With the Prussian in command of only one brief English profanity, Walker humorously recalled the sight of von Steuben running along the lines and bellowing, "Over here! Swear at him for me."[40]

---

[38] National Park Service

[39] Historic Valley Forge

[40] Historic Valley Forge

Pictures of the parade ground used to drill soldiers at Valley Forge

An illustration depicting von Steuben drilling soldiers

Despite the fact the Prussian baron had nothing in common with them, the American soldiers took well to von Steuben. Naturally, they had never encountered anyone like him in the colonies, and one soldier's account expressed awe at first seeing him, calling von Steuben the "perfect personification of Mars, the trappings of his horse, the enormous holsters of his pistols, and his shockingly martial aspect."[41] An important lesson von Steuben learned early at Valley Forge suggested that the American soldier was different than any other in terms of obedience. Respect of a soldier for his commanding officer was not automatic on the new continent, an unthinkable concept in the older countries of Europe. A Prussian would instantly risk his life over the most insignificant order, while an American would insist on an explanation before acting. If that explanation was deemed satisfactory, he would dutifully proceed. Such a quality was informed by the very nature of the struggle for independence, as Americans were in no mood to be directly ordered about by anyone without reason.

Von Steuben's "eclectic personality [was] greatly enhanced by his mystique,"[42] and soldiers responded well to the novelty of what they took to be a high-ranking European officer rubbing shoulders with American farmers and shopkeepers. For the most part, his fellow officers tended to view the infantrymen as a slave class, and foreigners of such rank often used them as one would a valet. In time, von Steuben came to inspire a general fondness among his men. He openly socialized with them on a rare occasion, and even the bluster came to be a source of merriment through the winter. The officers responded as well, as von Steuben's presence raised the general state of morale. Bringing humor to the desperate conditions, he staged a party for officers to parody his army's rag-tag condition. The requirement for attendance was wearing of torn clothing. Those with "a whole pair of breeches"[43] were to be turned away.

Once von Steuben's training approach became somewhat codified, Washington officially approved the regimen in late March 1778. Fully embracing the traditions of European discipline, von Steuben was nevertheless sensitive to American conditions and hurried the timetable along for coming battles. In his revision of the Prussian system, he sought to "incorporate American tactical experience" into present realities, originating in hunting practices and in response to America's specific terrain. As an antidote to sitting in the cold and sinking further into dejection, the men were constantly brought to their feet and ordered to march relentlessly. Von Steuben likewise continued to entertain the men through his quirky mannerisms and awkward attempts to introduce levity into the regimen. His heart was in his work, and the men loved his "sudden gusts of passion."[44] They watched in awe as von Steuben did the unthinkable by publicly apologizing to individual soldiers mistakenly called out for errors, hat in hand while standing in the rain.

When maneuvers were successful, he was of an "ebullient temperament"[45] bordering on

[41] National Park Service
[42] Historic Valley Forge
[43] Erin Blakemore
[44] North American Review
[45] Stephen C. Danckert

ecstasy, which caused no small amount of delight among the troops. Equally entertaining were his "hysterical rages"[46] as improvements became obvious throughout the army. Initial weapons drills that were first executed without muskets soon grew into a masterful display of carrying, loading, and aiming despite the constant turnover of personnel. The bayonet at last was integrated into the Continental Army's subconscious for both defense and charges. A hierarchical structure for which Washington had yearned took shape as well, with established tactical units. Battalions were collected from brigades of 1,000, and two brigades equaled a division. By the end of April, barely a month following Washington's approval of the training regimen, von Steuben's charges were able to precisely demonstrate all the skills and battlefield maneuvers on a grand scale. At last, he convinced the infantrymen and fellow officers that European marching drills were not merely ceremonial or a way to pass the time, but the only safe and effective way to wage combat in line formations against an experienced enemy.

For monitoring each unit, von Steuben's inspectors formed into their own tiers, including sub-inspectors for tracking the smallest matters. These included not only equipment and procedures, but also claims of illness and absenteeism. The inspectors of upper rank were selected by officers, and each had five sub-inspectors beneath him. Every excuse was investigated, and each musket was open to frequent inspections that included individual cartridges and knapsacks. The sergeant, often described as the backbone of the army, ably took over their small units in both combat and training.

With a rapidly improving armed force, von Steuben took matters further by tracking on paper the whereabouts and condition of every weapon on the field. Within a short time, every facet of military life was documented, with men reporting to sub-inspectors, who reported regularly to inspectors. From the time of his arrival, von Steuben sensed the presence of widespread "administrative incompetence, graft, [and] war profiteering"[47] present in the military structure, but thanks to his hierarchy of inspectors and insistence on detailed bookkeeping, an estimated 5,000-8,000 muskets were saved from neglect, misplacement, or theft. Such supervision translated into significant monetary savings, as the price of a single musket had reached $18 with the inclusion of a bayonet, and $16 without. An estimated figure of $200,000-$235,000 was recouped, and total estimates for recovered equipment grew to such profound proportions that in April, Washington recommended to Congress the creation of an Inspector General's office. He had considered creation of such an office for some time.

The establishment of the Inspector General's office with von Steuben installed as its head was made official on May 5, 1778. The baron was assigned to the post at a rank of Lieutenant Colonel, and as a bonus to his new capacity, he was rewarded with a house at Valley Forge for the duration of the encampment. His skills as a trainer and an organizer were so effective that his career course was taken in the opposite direction from what he had desired: a field command. He

[46] Stephen C. Danckert
[47] Russell Yost, Baron von Steuben Facts and Biography, The History Junkie – www.thehistoryjunkie.com/baron-von-steuben-facts/

continued to press for troops of his own to lead into battle, but Washington, keenly aware of his value, resisted.

Such success was not equally celebrated at all quarters. Continental officers grew disgruntled with Washington's growing admiration for foreign officers such as von Steuben and Lafayette despite their legitimate contributions. A pattern developed throughout the war as various figures jockeyed for promotions and threatened to resign until their tender feelings were soothed. Thankfully, with the exception of Benedict Arnold, few made good on such threats.

The winter at Valley Forge remains legendary in military history both for its severity and its results. In the end, the time that the American troops spent there proved to be critical to the future of the American colonies. While many died and others deserted, those that remained were closer to each other than they had ever been before, becoming true brothers in arms in a way that only privation and desperation could produce. Perhaps more importantly, von Steuben succeeded in transforming forces consisting mostly of inexperienced militia patched together into a professional army that could fight the British on open ground. The Prussian veteran would later note that the "enterprise succeeded better than…expected," and today the Valley Forge National Historical Park bills the site as "the birthplace of the United States Army."

Most arrived in the camp in December 1777 as Pennsylvanians or Virginians or New Yorkers, but they left in June 1778 as Americans, dedicated to a common cause that would unite them not just for the rest of the war but for the decades that followed. This dedication would see them through battles with bullets and with words, as each man, woman and child contributed their own part to creating the American dream. Before leaving their winter encampment, the officers who had survived took an oath that would shape all their future dealings, both as part of the army and of the new nation. Each man stated, in the presence of his peers, "I do acknowledge the UNITED STATES of AMERICA to be Free, Independent and Sovereign States, and declare that the people thereof owe no allegiance or obedience to George the Third, King of Great Britain ; and I renounce, refuse and abjure any allegiance or obedience to him; and I do Swear that I will, to the utmost of my power, support, maintain and defend the said United States against the said King George the Third, his heirs and successors, and his or their abettors, assistants and adherents, and will serve the said United States in the office of Lieutenant which I now hold, with fidelity, according to the best of my skill and understanding."

The End of the Revolution

Von Steuben's book of *Regulations*, affectionately known as the *Blue Book*, could not have come to the Continental Army at a better time. In the months leading up to Valley Forge, the British had retaken valuable strategic locations in every colony, and the tide was turning in their favor. The army of Valley Forge emerged from its worst winter as an effective and disciplined force, capable of meeting a traditional European military. Before the arrival of von Steuben, no American had an equivalent grasp of military quality as found in Prussia, but neither did most of the armies of Europe, including the British.

The impact of von Steuben's training was made clear on May 20, 1778, at the Battle of Barren Hill. A large British force attempted to encircle and capture a group of Continentals led by Marquis de Lafayette, whose force of 2,200 was outnumbered by more than 3-1. Lafayette learned of the ambush only the night before. Through "skillful maneuvering"[48] coordinated within a brief period, his force avoided entrapment. Indian scouts undertook a feint along with company cannons while the remainder escaped, following safely after. Within Lafayette's company was a large group of the "best Patriots,"[49] fresh off a grueling round of training under von Steuben at Valley Forge. Not a single life was lost.

By the summer of 1778, von Steuben was with Washington at the summer headquarters. In June, he nearly made good on his case to be given a field command for rescue actions taken at the Battle of Monmouth Courthouse in New Jersey. The British vacated Philadelphia, and to the Americans' surprise, sent a large contingent of troops and supplies overland through the New Jersey countryside. Washington saw this migration as a rich target, and on June 28, commands under several generals converged at Monmouth to attack vulnerable elements led by Sir Henry Clinton. The commands met the night before at the Englishtown Village Inn to finalize plans. Washington left that meeting believing that all the generals understood the orders. However, General Charles Lee had argued against the plan, and his loyalty was in doubt. In possession of the most disciplined troops he had ever commanded, thanks in large part to the von Steuben regimen, Washington moved on against British positions at Monmouth in consort with his generals. Lee, whose credentials were solid, and who had served armies in both Britain and Russia, mysteriously balked at the charge, claiming conflicting intelligence and estimates of resistance coming against him. Before long, he was in full retreat, which he allowed to continue without informing Washington. The British spotted Lee as the weak point on the filed and collapsed on him. Washington responded by relieving him of duty and replacing him in the field with von Steuben, who fended off catastrophe by halting the chaos and restoring order. In an instant, his men "rallied and wheeled"[50] as cleanly as they had on the parade grounds. By reorganizing themselves rapidly and under fire, von Steuben was able to salvage at least a partial victory by shoring up Lee's weak link. Lee never commanded again, and Washington was left with the benefit of knowing that von Steuben could offer quality leadership in the field.

In the following year, von Steuben's training manual proved itself once more in an action on the Hudson River. From New York, Clinton moved 8,000 British regulars up the river, capturing several points and barring the use of King's Ferry to the Americans. Surrounded by water on three sides, the British referred to Stony Point as their "little Gibraltar."[51] A garrison of 700

---

[48] History.com, This Day in History, May 20, Battle of Barren Hill, Pennsylvania – www.history.com/this-day-in-history/baattle-of-barren-hill
[49] History.com
[50] North American Review
[51] Kennedy Hickman, American Revolution: Battle of Stony Brook

British remained, but on July 16, 1779, General Anthony Wayne assaulted the position stealthily with 1,300 soldiers. Part of the area was flooded, and having to wade the last short distance alerted the British, but the Continentals captured almost 500 of the enemy and control of Stony Point without firing more than a minimal number of shots. By relying on the bayonet instead, von Steuben's drill regimen likely saved hundreds of lives on both sides.

The principles laid out by von Steuben in what came to be known affectionately as the *Blue Book* were soon adopted as a new way of life among Washington's troops, and they were formally published in 1779. Congress had returned to Philadelphia, and von Steuben was in residence nearby. Offering valuable assistance was Lt. Colonel Francois de Fleury, a French volunteer who penned the bulk of the original French text. Du Ponceau and Captain Walker translated the document into English. Added illustrations were the work of Captain Pierre Charles L'Enfant, who was later responsible for designing the capital city of Washington, D.C. The final printing was undertaken by Eleazer Oswald at The Coffee-House of Philadelphia, which was a difficult process as only two copper plates still existed in Philadelphia. The complete title, as the Army would first come to know it, was *Regulations for the Order and Discipline of the Troops of the United States*. Once distributed throughout the 13 colonies, it remained in use through the War of 1812. Pleased with the subsequent success created by such protocols, von Steuben took particular delight in his newfound ability to swear in seven different languages.

The *Blue Book* rested on seven principles demanding rigid adherence. The first was intended to solve the difficulty of recognizing rank in the field at a time when uniforms took the form of any style available to the individual soldier. Through Valley Forge, uniforms had been "pieced together."[52] By the instructions of the *Blue Book*, officers, non-commissioned officers, and infantrymen were standardized in dress, and all military garb clearly declared the rank of each man.

Next, the *Regulations* placed a heavy emphasis on marching orders and drills. A sizeable portion of the entire document was devoted to marching in formation in order to prepare for fighting in the same configuration. Coordinated wheeling motion and adjustments to enemy maneuvers without ensuing chaos took up the bulk of a soldier's typical day.

The third section offered a point-by-point instruction manual on cleanliness standards, the first order of which was to avoid digging a latrine near the preparation of food. This was, sadly, an astonishingly new idea to many of the men, because in their minds, the shortest distance between one and the other was the most convenient.

In the fourth section, von Steuben introduced the idea of meticulous bookkeeping to each unit

---

[52] Eric Milzarski, 7 Regulations from von Steuben's 'Blue Book' That Troops Still Follow, We are the Mighty – www.wearethemighty.com/military-culture/von-steuben-blue-book

in the Army, not satisfied to leave it in the hands of one or a small group of supervisors. The inclusion of careful paperwork was "paramount"[53] to success in keeping stock of equipment, a concept that was previously unused in the Continental Army. It was instituted with severe demands of accuracy on the individual, down to the smallest of items carried in the field. In making tactical decisions, the entire chain of command was required to know precisely what resources were at his command. Leading a charge with inaccurate resource estimates was an invitation to disaster, and punishment of incompetence in this arena was directed most harshly at the quartermaster, who would be fined until losses were recouped and errors resolved.

The fifth section concerned all matters connected to illness or injury suffered by any member of the unit. Non-commissioned officers were instructed to check the ranks of ill and wounded soldiers regularly, making detailed reports to the commanding officer each day. The tradition lives to the present day, as squad leaders report to the sergeant on the well-being of men in the infirmary each morning.

The subsequent section on non-commissioned officers highlights the importance of the rank, equally important to any other in the entire army. Following von Steuben's early efforts to train the model company personally, the NCO became the instructor, charged with teaching the infantryman "everything about what it means to be a soldier."[54] In the *Regulations*, the NCO is charged with tending to the well-being of each soldier under his command, even while functioning as a fully engaged soldier himself. Above all, he must lead from the front, regardless of the danger in which it might place him. He must reject all opportunities for comparative luxury or safety, and he cannot ask his men to do that which he is not also willing to do.

The final section of *Regulations* dealt with General Orders, covering a wide range of potential scenarios. The soldier is required, first and foremost, to guard everything within the confines of his post, and to remain at his post until properly relieved of duty. He is instructed to obey all special orders pertaining to any single situation that might occur outside of the customary regimen. Such orders are to be obeyed in a military manner which covers all areas of a soldier's performance while at his post. The soldier of even the lowliest rank is required to report all violations of orders that he might witness, regardless of the one violating the rule. He was instructed to report emergencies, and to be willing at all times to sound the general alarm if appropriate. This directive is relevant to any unanticipated possibility that might occur within General Orders.

In September 1780, von Steuben sat on the court-martial for the trial of British spy Major John André. No one who knew André personally would ever have dreamed he would one day hang. He was raised by devoutly religious parents and was a loyal Englishman and solid officer in His Majesty's Army. He had, it was rumored, an unfortunate romantic liaison that ended with a

---

[53] Eric Milzarski
[54] Eric Milzarski

cancelled engagement, and during the early days of the Revolutionary War, he had served his king in Canada before being captured and held as a prisoner of war. Once he was returned to his command, he was promoted in recognition of his strength of character under duress.

His reputation was so sterling, in fact, that he was given a very sensitive role, that of gathering intelligence for the British Army as they tried to put down the rebellious American colonies. This assignment, and an alleged relationship to a beautiful young Loyalist in Philadelphia named Peggy Shippen, would lead him to one of the colonists' biggest war heroes, Benedict Arnold. Arnold had arguably been more instrumental for the colonies' successes from 1775-1778 than anyone else, even perhaps George Washington, but a confluence of events left him willing to betray the cause he had fought and bled so hard for after he became military commander of Philadelphia.

In one of the most controversial and scrutinized episodes of the war, Arnold married Peggy Shippen despite her Loyalist sympathies, and while Arnold was willing to break the first rule, André broke the second rule by using Shippen to pass messages, possibly even playing on her own affections for him.

A self-portrait of André

Ultimately, it was in breaking the third rule of espionage that André made his fatal mistake, for when he met near West Point to facilitate Arnold's betrayal, he changed his clothes one fateful night in September 1780. When André was caught in the field by irregular forces, Arnold used the very boat intended for André, the *Vulture*, to make his getaway. Had he not been caught in civilian clothing, André would not have been considered a spy but instead an enemy combatant and therefore a prisoner of war. Arnold, on the other hand, knew that he did not stand a chance if caught.

Respecting Washington as a man of honor, André believed that he might find mercy in him. Hamilton observed, "The first step he took after his capture, was to write a letter to General Washington, conceived in terms of dignity without insolence, and apology without meanness. The scope of it was to vindicate himself from the imputation of having assumed a mean character, for treacherous or interested purposes; asserting that he had been involuntarily an imposter; that contrary to his intention, which was to meet a person for intelligence on neutral ground, he had been betrayed within our posts, and forced into the vile condition of an enemy in disguise…"

Whatever his personal feelings on the matter, Washington knew he had to proceed against André according to military rules. Tallmadge later reported, "I took on Major André, under a strong escort of cavalry, to West Point, and the next day I proceeded down the Hudson to King's Ferry, and landed at Haverstraw, on the West side of the Hudson, where a large escort of cavalry had been sent from the main army at Tappan, with which I escorted the prisoner to Head-Quarters. After we arrived at Head-Quarters, I reported myself to Gen. Washington, who ordered a court consisting of fourteen general officers, to sit and hear the case of Major André."

André's trial began on September 29, 1780, with instructions written by Washington. Its contents were decidedly neutral: "Major André, Adjutant General to the British army, will be brought before you for your examination. He came within our lines in the night, on an interview with Major General Arnold, and in an assumed character; and was taken within our lines, in a disguised habit, with a pass under a feigned name, and with the enclosed papers concealed upon him. After a careful examination, you will be pleased, as speedily as possible, to report a precise state of his cafe, together with your opinion of the light in which he ought to be considered, and the punishment that ought to be inflicted. The Judge Advocate will attend to assist in the examination, who has sundry other papers relative to this matter, which he will lay before the Board."

What is thinly hidden in Washington's words is his respect for the captive. The general understood André was a major who was serving his country and had been caught dressed out of uniform due to a series of chance events. There was nothing in his attitude toward André that in any way rivaled his disdain for Arnold, who had played the part of traitor. At the same time, it was understood on both sides that Clinton could not and would not exchange Arnold for André, because doing so would obviously discourage others from switching sides to the British. As a result, the man both sides respected would be the one to hang. Von Steuben reined in his passions and carefully considered the case at trial. He understood that spy activities in wartime could be among the most dangerous to a defending army, and Andre was hanged as a spy behind American lines "under a feigned name and in a disguised habit"[55] on October 2, 1780. Hamilton himself remarked with a hint of bitterness not only that André had to die, but that he had to die in the manner befitting a spy, not a military officer: "Never, perhaps, did any man suffer death with more justice, or deserve it less."

In the months leading up to the Continental Army's move south, von Steuben became Washington's strongest representative before Congress, in tandem with the constant flow of letters to Philadelphia from the commanding general. Von Steuben's presence as a spokesman was largely devoted to the reorganization of the Continental Army, from the progress of the training regimen to the constant threat of officer resignations which at times caused widespread inconvenience to the cause.

As the British emphasis shifted to the South, where they hoped for a greater upsurge of loyalist support, von Steuben prepared to move south as well under the command of Nathanael Greene, in support of General John Sullivan as a supply officer and in charge of training for the southern troops. Instructions and equipment from Congress were customarily slow, but von Steuben spent the time wisely, doing the same for the Virginians as he had for the men at Valley Forge. With meager resources, he was able to reasonably outfit the men, including uniforms for clarification of rank. Meeting with each of the colonels commanding troops in the region, he ordered them to dispense with their individual systems, which understandably met with some resistance. As before, the ability to fight in line formation was absent. Starting at the beginning, he took them through the *Regulations*, and he finished off the combat portion by teaching the proper etiquette for greeting guest dignitaries (now that the French were fully engaged in the war effort). As a supply officer, von Steuben continued his duties in support of Sullivan and Greene, usually with a "lack of men, of materials, and civilian support."[56]

Even after his successful transformation of the Continental Army at Valley Forge and the dissemination of the *Regulations*, von Steuben continued to face much resentment for being a foreigner. The term carried a different meaning in the colonial era, as almost everyone was a foreigner, or from foreign parents, but those of British heritage claimed the mantle of membership within the new nation, whereas a recently-arrived Prussian was a threat to high-ranking military employment. Still desirous of a command post, von Steuben carried his own resentment when Lafayette was sent instead. Von Steuben had fought in the trenches at the Siege of Prague 13 years before Lafayette was born, he had developed a reputation as a soldier, and he had trained at the feet of 18th century Europe's greatest general. Conversely, Lafayette had purchased his rank through personal wealth and connections to French royalty. The Frenchman

[55] USHistory.org
[56] Allen French

had only come under fire a few occasions, which, according to von Steuben, brought him an unmerited "affectionate reverence"[57] that should have been the Prussian baron's. Where Lafayette was "mercurial,"[58] von Steuben was "dignified and punctilious."[59] Lafayette was ideologically passionate, but von Steuben put on the American uniform "as he would have a uniform of Austria or Sardinia, for higher rank."[60] The final indignity, although von Steuben might not have openly expressed it, was that Lafayette was French, not German or Prussian.

As a result, by June 1781, von Steuben was delivering 450 newly trained Continentals to Lafayette, and while the epic actions of Savannah, Charleston, and Camden were taking place, von Steuben remained in Virginia attending to those tasks for which he was renowned and most appreciated.

Circumstances in the South were driving Lord Cornwallis northward toward Virginia, and Washington did him the final courtesy of offering von Steuben a command at the British general's surrender at Yorktown. The loss of Cornwallis was a crushing blow to Britain, and although the war went on for a while longer, the end of the British involvement was inevitable. As one of three American commanders present at Yorktown, von Steuben was the only officer among them who had ever witnessed a true siege. It was to be the first and last time he would command a division.

---

[57] North American Review

[58] North American Review

[59] North American Review

[60] North American Review

Von Steuben's Final Years

A portrait of von Steuben

Two years following the surrender of Cornwallis, von Steuben assisted a grateful Washington in the demobilization of the army. No longer the Continental Army, it was rebranded as the new U.S. Army.

In July 1783, Congress sent von Steuben in his capacity of Inspector General to the Canadian frontier. There, he reclaimed American possession of formerly British posts. In the same month, he prepared for a return to Europe, where he expected to be well received, but his request for French citizenship and a military assignment with full pay was brushed aside by the French Ministry with "polite indifference."

Returning to North America in December of the same year, von Steuben attended Washington's farewell party at Fraunces Tavern in New York City before moving on to Philadelphia to settle accounts with Congress. However, regardless of the arrangement for full payment following a successful resolution, the new country had a broken economy, and where funds were not available, Congress substituted what they could. The first tract offered to von Steuben was a New Jersey house 15 miles from New York City, confiscated from a Loyalist named Jan Zabriskie. Given full ownership of the house, Congress declared that von Steuben could "hold, occupy, and enjoy the said estate in person, and not by tenant."[61]

Von Steuben was hesitant to accept such payment once hearing of the circumstances under which it was attained, and he went so far as to intercede on Zabriskie's behalf. The abuses of war had rendered the estate barely habitable, despite the fact Washington had used it as a headquarters for a time in 1780, but von Steuben ultimately took it on in full knowledge that it would not be returned to Zabriskie under any circumstance. The former owner, in turn, sued the British government for compensation.

Elisa Rolle's picture of the house

Pennsylvania soon came through with an offer of American citizenship for von Steuben, a gesture seconded by New York soon after in the spring of 1784. Von Steuben, not yet sure of his fate if he returned to Europe, settled down to see what could be done with the Zabriskie house, which included a grist mill, an orchard, a large patch of meadow ground, and a large supply of wood. Close to New York, he had access by boat to an ample supply of oysters, fish, and waterfowl.

Still not finding the situation suitable, he settled soon after in Yorktown, New York where he

---

[61] Kevin W. Wright

became a fixture in the community. At one point back in Europe, von Steuben had been forced to convert to Catholicism, but he now served as an Elder at the Reformed German Church at 131 Norfolk Street. A plaque at the site commemorates the baron, crediting him for "fulfilling the decrees of Heaven" by helping achieve the independence of the United States."[62] In Yorktown, he was visited by a contingent of German relatives who celebrated his role in the Revolution.

Despite living as a prominent figure in his new town, von Steuben was never a good businessman, and he lived the rest of his life dealing with financial difficulties. He lived from month to month hoping the U.S. government would come through with final payments. For a time, he took up temporary lodgings in Philadelphia while he performed his final duties as the Inspector General. When he tendered his resignation to Congress, a reminder was included that he was owed $8,500 for his services. In the end, he received $1,700 and a treasury note bearing interest at 6%. With the economy not yet on its feet, he was unable to sell the note for 10% of its worth. In a flourish of gratitude, Congress presented him with a gold-hilted sword as well. Still destitute, von Steuben eventually sold his favorite horse and a set of tableware to remain afloat.

In July 1786, von Steuben was discharged from the military. At that time, he received a letter from General Gates, the victor of Saratoga who had been disgraced after the loss at Camden. Not prone to warm gestures, Gates declared that "my great respect for you will not end with the war."[63]

As financial conditions worsened, von Steuben placed his finances under Benjamin Walker, and he eventually moved in with Walker's family and William North of his former staff. After modernizing the New Jersey estate to habitability, he promptly sold it. The following day, it was repurchased by Jan Zabriskie's son.

In June 1790, von Steuben was granted an annual pension of $2,500. Alexander Hamilton and various friends assisted him with what was termed a "friendly mortgage"[64] for a 16,000 acre tract and cabin in the Mohawk Valley of Oneida County. The baron took a turn at farming, which he studied in the same manner with which he had studied war. During this period, he remained close to Walker and North, and the three were said to have led their own particular brand of romantic relationship for some years. Same-sex relationships were more "widely tolerated"[65] until the evangelical religious movements of the following century swept the continent. Although same-sex marriage was far from becoming legalized, a common practice of the era was for men to adopt one another, which von Steuben did in the case of Walker and North. The joint sentiment of the two men expressed itself fully by declaring, "We love him, and he deserves it for he loves us tenderly."[66] The thoughts of the wives and children of both men are largely unknown, but the

---

[62] Wayne Johnson, Baron von Steuben, *Leben, A Journal of Reformation Life*, Oct. 1, 2005 – www.leben.us/baron-von-steuben/

[63] Dana W. Bigelow, Baron von Steuben at Home at Rest in Oneida County, *Proceedings of the New York Historical Association* Vol. 14 (1915) pp91-100

[64] Historic Valley Forge

[65] Erlin Blakemore

[66] Erin Blakemore

baron never married and never had children.

According to Rufus Wilmot Griswold, in his *Republican Court*, von Steuben assembled a congress of the handsomest officers on the continent that came to be known, affectionately or otherwise, as "Captain Harsin's New York Grenadiers." These men were known by their "blue coats with red facings and gold lace embroideries, cocked hats with white feathers, white waistcoats and breeches…black spatterdashes buttoned close from the shoe to the knee."[67] Von Steuben's contingent was among those standing guard at the inauguration of George Washington as the first President of the United States. The unmarried baron continued to sell portions of various acreage given to him by Congress for survival.

Few saw him in his last months, with his only public appearance being in the capacity as President of the German Society in New York. He lived his last days virtually alone, as the cabin was isolated by several waterfalls, making water transportation to his land impossible.

On November 28, 1794, Friedrich Wilhelm von Steuben died at the age of 64 in his cabin in the Mohawk Valley. On the day of his death, he became paralyzed in the morning, and he was dead by noon. He died, impoverished, in a crude log house in the midst of the wilderness. Von Steuben was buried with minimal ceremony in a pine coffin, wrapped in his military cloak, and interred in a place "designated in advance by himself."[68] His burial was attended by Benjamin Walker, but no marker existed. Years later, his remains were exhumed and relocated for the construction of a road through the area. Von Steuben's grave is now located at the Steuben Memorial State Heroic Site.

---

[67] Homohistory.com, Friedrich Wilhelm von Steuben, Gay Revolutionary War Hero, May 24, 2014 – www.homohistory.com/2014/05/friedrich-wilhelm-von-steuben-gay_24.html

[68] Dana W. Bigelow

Doug Kerr's picture of von Steuben's grave

As a bachelor with no immediate family, he left the bulk of his assets to William North and Benjamin Walker. To John Mulligan, his aide and secretary, he left his personal library and an undisclosed amount of money. Three wills were left behind, two of which were preserved for posterity. The first was written in 1777, prior to his departure for America, and is enshrined in the archives of Hohenzollern-Hechingen. A second will in 1781 was drawn up a few months before the end of the war. It is housed in the Oneida Historical Society.

Many monuments have commemorated von Steuben as a symbol of the fight for independence, and many communities across America have expressed pride in him. The NYPD Steuben Association of New York represents the pride of police officers of German and Austrian descent. Many communities schedule a Von Steuben Day in the month of September, and in many locations, that celebration is the largest German-American event of the year. The Steuben Parade is to the present day a well-attended event in New York City and Chicago. In 1919, the Steuben Society was founded, and many military craft on land and sea bear his name, not to mention an ocean liner. Several cities used him as a namesake, such as Steubenville, Ohio.

Likewise, various items and memorials connected to von Steuben abound in Europe. The Castle of Hohenzollern, home of the Hohenzollern dynasty, is said to possess "a wealth of

Prussian artifacts,"[69] including a personal letter from George Washington in praise of von Steuben's meritorious service to the new United States.

As with any public historic figure, von Steuben has both admirers and critics. One temperate description characterizes him as a "pleasant and able soldier,"[70] but few descriptions remain so moderate. One critic assesses him as a "precise Martinet, a perfect Prussian,"[71] a dreamer who indulged all available appetites without consideration or remorse. The author goes on to classify von Steuben as more of a courtier than a soldier, and one who took up the American cause to avoid arrest on the European continent. Some criticize his personal life, which they claimed was too preoccupied with assembling a group of men around him, as his godfather and mentor, Frederick the Great, had done in Berlin.

That said, despite some modern articles speculating on his sexuality, von Steuben's life and legacy have been upheld by respected authors. John McAuley Palmer referred to him as a "military father"[72] who was not in the least opposed to the traditional family. Allegedly an "interesting and delightful person"[73] who was unable to live within his means, he possessed the talent "to touch the pocket of friends."[74]

Indeed, Baron von Steuben gave Washington the army he desired, codified a manual of training with principles that still serve in the modern day, and helped make the "sergeant…the most important soldier in the army."[75] In his own time, the Prussian soldier with the heavily fabricated past proved to be "indispensable to the achievement of American independence,"[76] and he is rightly celebrated across his adopted country over 200 years after his death.

Online Resources

Other Revolutionary Era titles by Charles River Editors

Other titles about Baron von Steuben on Amazon

Further Reading

Bigelow, Dana W. Baron von Steuben at home, at Rest, in Oneida (1915), *Proceeding of the New York Historical Association*, Vol. 14

Blakemore, Erin, The Revolutionary War Hero Who Was Openly Gay, History.com, June 14,

---

[69] Inspirock, Castle of Hohenzollern-Hechingen – www.inspirock.com/germany/hechingen/castle-of-hohenzollern-0119860853

[70] Kevin W. Wright

[71] Bobarnebeck.com, Baron von Steuben – www.bobarnebeck.com/baron.html

[72] Bobarnebeck.com

[73] Allen French

[74] Allen French

[75] Dr. Robert H. Bouilly, *Army University Press*

[76] North American Review

2018 – www.history.com/news/openly-gay-war-hero-friedrich-von-steuben

Bobarnebeck.com, Baron von Steuben – www.bobarnebeck.com/baron.html

Bonham, M.L., Review of Friedrich Wilhelm von Steuben and the American Revolution of Joseph Doyle, *The Mississippi Valley Historical Review*, Vol. 1 No. 1 (June, 1914) Oxford University Press

Bouilly, Robert H., Dr., The American Revolution and the NCO Tradition, *Army University Press*, Oct. 16, 2017

Danckert, Stephen C., A Genius for Training, Baron von Steuben and the Training of the Continental Army, *Army History*, No. 17 (Winter 1990/1991) Army Center of Military History

Durham, J. Lloyd, Outfitting an American Revolutionary Soldier, NCPedia, North Carolina Museum of History, 1992 – www.ncpedia.org/history/usrevolution/soldiers

Encyclopaedia Britannica, Baron Steuben, German Military Officer – www.britannica.com/biography/Baron-von-Steuben

Eyewitness to History.com, The Continental Army at Valley Forge, 1777 – www.eyewitnesstohistory.com/valleyforge.htm

French, Allen, Review of John McAuley Palmer, General von Steuben, *The American Historical Review* Vol. 43 No. 4 (July, 1938)

Friedrich Wilhelm von Steuben Quotes – www.quotes.com/author/S1040-Friedrich_Wilhelm_von_Steuben

Hickman. Kennedy, American Revolution: Battle of Stony Point, Thoughtco., March 17, 2017 – www.thoughtco.com/battle-of-stony-point-2360641

Historic Valley Forge, Baron von Steuben, History.org – www.history.org/valleyforge/served/steuben.html

History.com, This Day in History, Mary 20, Battle of Barren Hill, Pennsylvania – www.history.com/this-day-in-history/battle-of-barren-hill

Homohistory.com, Friedrich Wilhelm von Steuben, Gay Revolutionary War Hero, May 24, 2014 – www.homohistory.om/2014/05/friedrich-wilhelm-von-Steuben-gay_24.html

Inspirock.com, Castle of Hohenzollern-Hechingen – www.inspirock.com/germany/hechingen/castle-of-hohenzollern-a119860853

Johnson Wayne, Baron von Steuben, *Leben, A Journal of Reformation Life*, Oct. 1, 2005 – www.leven.us/baron-von-stuben/

Military Wikia.com/wiki/Friedrich_Wilhelm_von_Steuben

Milzarski, Eric, We Are the Mighty, 7 Regulations from von Steuben's 'Blue Book' That Troops Still Follow – wearethemighty.com/military-culture/von-steuben-blue-book

Mount Vernon.org, Baron von Steuben – www.mountvernon.org/library/digitalhistory/digital-encylopedia/rtile/baron-von-steuben/

National Park Service, Valley Forge, General von Steuben – www.nps.gov/valleyforge/learn/historyculture/vonsteuben.html

North American Review, Review of Friedrich Kapp's The Life of Frederick von Steuben,, Major-General in the Revolutionary Army, *The North American Review*, Vol. 99 No. 205 (Oct., 1864), University of Northern Iowa

Palmer, John McAuley Palmer, Franklin's Patriotic Fib, *The North American Review*, Vol. 233, No. 6 (June, 1932)

Paperdue.com. Baron von Steuben, Friedrich Wilhelm Augustus von Essay – www.paperdue.com/baron-von-steuben-friedrich-wilhelm-augustus-84489

Pavao, Esther, Baron von Steuben, Revolutionary War.net – www.revolutionarywar.net/baron-von-steuben.html

Reese, Charles Jr., Review of John McAuley Palmer's General von Steuben, *The Pennsylvania Magazine of History and Biography*, Vol. 62 No. 1 (Jan., 1938)

Review of The Life of Friedrich Wilhelm von Steuben, Major General in the Revolutionary Army of Friedrich Kapp, *The North American Review*, Vol. 99 No. 205 (Oct., 1864), University of Northern Iowa

Segal, Mark, Baron Friedrich Wilhelm von Steuben, The Closet Professor – www.closetprofessor.blogspot.com/2016/07/baron-friedrich-wilhelm-von-steuben.html

Segal, Mark, Friedrich von Steuben: Father of the U.S. Military, Blade, Oct. 19, 2011 – www.washingtonblade.com/2011/10/19/friedrich-von-steuben-father-of-the-us-military

Still, James, The Post & Mail, Baron von Steuben (1778), Feb. 1, 2018 – www.thepostmail.com/2018/02/01/baron-von-steuben-1778/

Study.com, Baron von Steuben – www.study.com/academy/lesson/baron-von-steuben-quotes-facts-biography.html

Thoughtco., American Revolution: Baron Friedrich von Steuben – www.thoughtco.com/baron-friedrich-von-steuben-2360603

Trickey, Erick, Smithsonian.com, The Prussian Nobleman Who Helped Save the American Revolution, April 26, 2017 – www.smithsonianmag.com/history/baron-on-steuben-1809663048/

USHistory.org, Major John Andre – www.history.org/march/bio/andre.htm

Wiki Visually, Friedrich Wilhelm von Steuben – wikivisually.com/wiki/Friedrich_Wilhelm_von_Steuben

Wright, Kevin W., Bergen County Historical Society, Friedrich Wilhelm Steuben – www.bergencoungtyhistory.org/Pages/gnsteuben.html

Yost, Russell, Baron von Steuben Facts and Biography, the History Junkie – www.thehistoryjunkie.com/baron-von-steuben-fats/

Free Books by Charles River Editors

We have brand new titles available for free most days of the week. To see which of our titles are currently free, click on this link.

Discounted Books by Charles River Editors

We have titles at a discount price of just 99 cents everyday. To see which of our titles are currently 99 cents, click on this link.

Made in the USA
Monee, IL
19 August 2024